- Crocuses and Tulips blooming in winter

- Apple or grapefruit plants from seed

- Brilliant-colored Coleuses

- Feathery Asparagus Ferns

- Tiny tropical plants in a terrarium

All these delightful plants and many more are easy to grow indoors if you follow the instructions in this "how to" guide to the fun of indoor gardening!

KIDS' INDOOR GARDENING
was originally published by
Doubleday & Company, Inc.

Critics' Corner:

"A book that gives good coverage, sensible advice, and an encouraging word to the beginning gardener."

—*Bulletin of the Center for Children's Books,*
University of Chicago

"A most basic how-to book, *Kids' Indoor Gardening* delivers step-by-step, concise instructions for successful indoor gardening in a format easily followed by both adults and children."

—*Horticulture*

"Aileen Paul, author of *Kids Cooking,* has again demonstrated her ability to make instruction enjoyable for children with *Kids' Indoor Gardening,* a first indoor gardening book for the young. . . . The joy of watching and tending plants planted 'by myself' is common to all gardeners, no matter what their ages. Children, and especially today's urban children, should be introduced to it."

—*Natural Gardening*

About the Author and Illustrator:

AILEEN PAUL has also written *Kids Camping* and co-authored *Kids Cooking,* both of which are available in Archway Paperback editions. She is an active on-the-air performer for television and radio, appearing on such shows as "Wonderama" and WNYC's "Children's Center"; a cooking and gardening teacher for children in New Jersey; a writer; and an adviser on banking for women for the New York State Banking Association. In 1973, Ms. Paul won the SESAC (Society of European Stage Authors and Composers) "AM Broadcaster of the Year" award from the President of the New York Chapter of American Women in Radio and Television (AWRT). She lives in New Jersey with her husband and three children, a German shepherd, and two parakeets.

ARTHUR HAWKINS graduated from the University of Virginia. He has designed numerous books, over 1,000 book jackets, and is the co-author of *Kids Cooking.* He is married, with four children.

KIDS' INDOOR GARDENING

(Original title: *Kids Gardening: A First Indoor Gardening Book for Children*)

written by Aileen Paul illustrated by Arthur Hawkins

AN ARCHWAY PAPERBACK
POCKET BOOKS • NEW YORK

KIDS' INDOOR GARDENING

Doubleday edition published 1972

Archway Paperback edition published January, 1975

Published by
POCKET BOOKS, a division of Simon & Schuster, Inc.,
A GULF+WESTERN COMPANY
630 Fifth Avenue, New York, N.Y. 10020.

Archway Paperback editions are distributed in the
U.S. by Simon & Schuster, Inc., 630 Fifth Avenue,
New York, N.Y. 10020, and in Canada by Simon &
Schuster of Canada, Ltd., Markham, Ontario, Canada.

ISBN: 0-671-29608-6.
Library of Congress Catalog Card Number: 73-177239.
This Archway Paperback edition is published by arrangement
with Doubleday & Company, Inc. Copyright, ©, 1972, by
Doubleday & Company, Inc. All rights reserved. *Kids' Indoor
Gardening* was originally published under the title *Kids
Gardening: A First Indoor Gardening Book for Children.*
This book, or portions thereof, may not be reproduced by
any means without permission of the original publisher:
Doubleday & Company, Inc., 277 Park Avenue,
New York, N.Y. 10017.

Printed in the U.S.A.

2376

dedication

To my mother, EDNA SAMUELSON DE GROFFT, who took me on evening walks through pastures and woods gathering Wild Iris and Columbine, and to my father, JOHN PRESTON PHILLIPS, who encouraged me, even as a small child, to share his gardening.

contents

a word to kids

The gardening world is a wonderful world. You can grow flowering plants like Geraniums, interesting foliage like Pickaback Plants, and unusual cacti such as Flowering Thorn. You can visit florists and greenhouses and plant sections in other stores. You can obtain helpful seed catalogs with pictures.

Much of the fun of gardening is in trial and error. You can not "get it all out of a book," as some people say, although you should know enough to get started when you have read this book. I can tell you in general terms what plants need to live, but gardening is really between you and your plants. Remember that plants are living things, and that they must be treated as individuals.

You will have problems from time to time, everyone does. You will kill a few plants, even experienced gardeners do. Don't be discouraged. Find out, if you can, where you went wrong so you can avoid repeating the same error, and start again.

So why not look at the plants in your neighborhood florist or dime store, and start with one or two. You'll have fun, I promise you, and plants will become a part of your life.

a word to adults

Thousands of years ago when men and women first learned to cultivate plants, they took a giant step forward, an achievement almost greater than going to the moon. For the first time they had a little power over their environment.

In these days when 70 per cent of America lives in urban areas, both adults and children have gotten a long way from the world of growing things. Food comes pre-packaged, flowers come ready cut, in bunches of six. So for a child, growing plants indoors can be more than a pleasant hobby. It is a way to get in touch with the basic patterns of nature. There are lessons of ecology to be learned from repotting a plant that can be applied to large trees and natural growth.

But in addition, what is important to each of us is the vital nonverbal communication

11

that takes place in the sharing of gardening activity when, for example, one gives a cutting from a favorite plant to a friend. There is also a unique pleasure when the first green sprouts appear at the top of a dull-looking Narcissus bulb and later when the fragrant flower appears. We are sure that this magic will occur, but there is a sense of fulfillment, a sense of renewal each time. And it is very important for children to be in touch with that kind of feeling, in the noisy, tense modern world in which we live.

Aside from providing somewhere for the beginning gardener to work (somewhere, incidentally, with a washable floor, for soil has a way of getting spread around) there isn't much advice I can give you. From my own experience of working with youngsters, I find that they need comparatively little supervision, perhaps some help in arranging for the few tools and items necessary.

KIDS' INDOOR GARDENING is not intended to be *a complete* book on gardening, but it is a basic guide to start beginning gardeners on their way.

chapter 1

getting started

Plants are bought at garden shops, florists, nurseries, and greenhouses. You can often purchase them, at a lower price, at dime stores and supermarkets.

Bulbs and seeds may be bought at garden shops and nurseries and, frequently, at hardware, grocery, and dime stores.

Among the large garden supply companies like W. Atlee Burpee Company, Philadelphia, Pennsylvania 19132, George W. Parks Seed Company, Inc., Greenwood, South Carolina 29646, and Jackson & Perkins Co., Medford, Oregon 97501, several offer house plants as well as bulbs and seeds. Write for a free catalog. You will find it helpful in many ways.

Look at the horticultural and garden magazines at the library. There will be mention of other plant and garden suppliers who have additional information available.

soil and containers

You can grow single plants or small indoor gardens successfully by following advice on the right soil, appropriate containers, and loving care.

soil

The right soil is necessary for indoor gardening. By *right soil,* we mean soil, not dirt.

You can buy a potting soil mixture, ready-mixed and sterilized. Most commercial prepared mixtures, however, are too fine. Add 1 part coarse perlite to 3 parts soil. Mix thoroughly and you have an acceptable basic potting soil.

You can prepare your own basic potting soil which we call mixture #1 with perlite, sphagnum peat moss ("brown" peat moss), bone meal, ground limestone, and top soil obtained from a nursery shop or your own garden.

To give you an idea of how much soil you will need, keep in mind that a 4-inch pot (a good size for many plants) takes slightly over 2 cups of soil.

Some experts feel it is necessary to use sterilized soil in preparing a potting mixture—that is, soil in which there are no harmful insects and diseases. While that may be desirable, I feel you will find it easier to use quality top soil without sterilizing. Should you want to sterilize soil, however, the easiest way is to bake it; and the only problem is that some strange odors may come out of the oven.

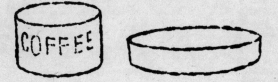

TO STERILIZE GARDEN SOIL

here's what you need

Several shallow containers (throw-away aluminum broiler pans are helpful)

Garden top soil

here's what you do

1. Turn oven to 180° F.

2. Spread soil very thinly in one or several containers.

3. Place containers in oven for 30 minutes.

4. Cool before using.

TO PREPARE POTTING MIXTURE NO. 1 (basic)

here's what you need

2 cups top soil

2 cups perlite

2 cups moistened brown peat moss

3 teaspoons bone meal

1 teaspoon ground limestone

Measuring cup or ordinary cup

Large container (such as bucket or 2-pound coffee can)

Stick or wooden spoon

here's what you do

1. Pour top soil, perlite, and peat moss into large container.

2. You now have 6 cups of potting mixture, and you can add the bone meal and limestone.

3. Mix thoroughly.

This soil mixture is suitable for most of the plants you will be growing.

> NOTE: Moisten brown peat moss by placing it in a fairly large bowl or bucket of warm water. Work the water into the peat moss with your hands, and then wring the surplus water out.

TO PREPARE POTTING MIXTURE NO. 2

A drier mixture is needed by succulents like Crown of Thorns, Sand Dollar, Century Plant, Aloe, Air Plant, and Jade Plant. Or any members of the cactus family.

here's what you need

1 cup top soil

2 cups perlite

here's what you do

1. Pour perlite and soil into a large container.

2. Mix thoroughly with stick or wooden spoon.

TO PREPARE
POTTING MIXTURE NO. 3

Plants with large foliage and a heavy root system such as Rubber Plants and Aspidistras do better in a heavier soil.

here's what you need

3 cups moistened brown garden soil

1 cup peat moss

1 cup perlite

2½ teaspoons bone meal

here's what you do

1. Pour soil, peat moss, and perlite into large container.

2. Add bone meal.

3. Mix thoroughly.

containers

Each plant container must have drainage (see page 23) so that excess water will drain off. The worst thing you can do to a plant is to let it stand with its feet wet.

TO BUY

You can buy clay or plastic pots which have drainage holes. They come in various sizes—from 2 inches up to 6 inches are generally used. The size is the distance inside the rim. Most plants grow well in 4-inch pots. A large plant (4 or 5 feet tall) can grow comfortably in a 6-inch pot. Some plants, however, like to be crowded.

You might buy used pots at a garden or nursery shop. Of course it would be nice if you were given used ones by friends or neighbors. Old pots should be thoroughly scrubbed. New clay pots should be soaked at least an hour in water and then allowed to dry.

TO FIND CONTAINERS

There is a source for containers other than shops, and that is in your own kitchen. Look for plastic containers such as those that ice cream and cottage cheese come in, empty milk cartons which you can cut down to 6 or 8 inches, coffee cans, or metal cookie boxes. If containers are flexible, handle carefully to avoid bruising roots.

Wash containers with soap and water (be particularly careful with those that have had milk products) and dry.

Punch 2 or 3 small holes in the bottom for drainage, either with a large nail, metal drill, or screw driver.

TO PREPARE FOR PLANTING

To prepare any container, make certain that drainage holes will not become plugged. There are two ways:

1. Place small piece of screening (new patches of screening can be bought at hardware stores) over drainage holes or holes in container.

or

2. Position small pieces of broken clay pots, curved side toward the top (umbrella fashion) over hole.

In either case, cover with shallow layer of small stones or gravel. If possible, place

1-inch layer of sphagnum moss over drainage material.

DRIP CATCHERS

Drip catchers are essential for containers of any sort so that no moisture rings are left on window sills, shelves, or tables.

Many pots come with their own drip catcher.

Drip catchers may be painted tin coffee-can lids, plastic tops from containers, saucers, plates, platters, or large metal trays for planters.

TO MAKE CONTAINERS MORE ATTRACTIVE

You can paint *metal* containers with enamel paint, before planting.

You can wrap containers and pots loosely with attractive colored foil, decorated paper, or crumpled aluminum foil.

And, possibly the best idea of all, place a smaller plain pot or container in a slightly larger attractive ceramic pot without drainage.

PLANTERS

If you decide to group your plants in an attractive planter or moisture-proof window box, they will probably grow better and they will make a pretty massed effect. Of course, you will put plants together that like the same amount of light, water, and temperature.

There are three ways of handling planters:

1. Sprinkle layer of pebbles or small rocks on bottom and fill planter with moisture-holding substance like peat moss or coarse perlite and sink clay pots in to rim level. Keep filler material moist and plants will need less direct watering.

2. Place 1 inch of clean small rocks or sand in planter. Add water almost to top level of rocks or sand, and group

pots directly on material. Pots should not touch water or the roots of the plants will rot. The moisture arising from the water helps plants stay healthy.

3. Spinkle layer of pebbles or small rocks on bottom and fill planter with soil.

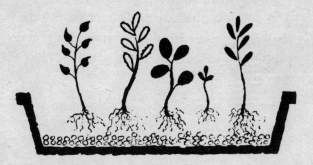

Remove plants from pots and follow instructions on page 23 for repotting. The disadvantage of this method is that the root system of the other plants is disturbed if you need to replace a plant.

WINDOW BOXES

I am reluctant to suggest the purchase of wooden window boxes, even if you can find a convenient size. The price is relatively high because the wood must be properly treated and there must be a removable metal liner.

There are small plastic or aluminum window boxes suitable for indoor use. Keep in mind the need for adequate drainage.

I think however you will find planters easier to handle and equally attractive for your indoor garden.

WHERE TO BUY
PLANTERS

Of course you can buy planters at garden shops, dime stores, hardware stores, and from catalog shops or seed growers by mail or directly.

You may, however, find large square or rectangular containers to use for planters in your kitchen or closet. One that I particularly like for small plants (a former cake storage pan) measures 9 inches square. Another favorite is a large wooden nut dish which we line with Saran Wrap or aluminum foil.

I like to search for planters in thrift shops (the type of musty-looking old stores that sell secondhand clothes and furniture). It's great fun to look for the unusual such as extra-large soup tureens, old-fashioned oversized brass cooking pots and roasting pans, even big ceramic bowls. One of my most successful planters, handsome and streamlined, is a long narrow aluminum fish-poacher with a take-out tray.

Rummage sales and auctions are another excellent source of planters.

once you have started (care of indoor plants)

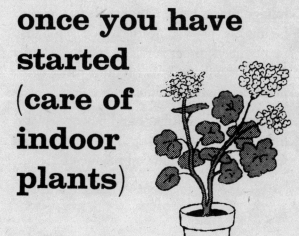

When you get your plants, remember they are living things that need good care. They need:

Light

Correct temperature

Moisture and fresh air

Watering

Feeding

plants need light

All plants need some light to grow. Most foliage plants can be grown near windows facing east or even north. Flowering house plants need direct sunlight several hours a day. You will find instructions for specific plants on the following pages.

Plants turn their foliage and flowers toward light. So give plants a half turn once a week to keep shape well balanced.

Artificial light is discussed on page 109.

temperature is important

Most house plants grow best in an even, moderate temperature from 60° to 70° F.

During very cold weather, move plants back from window so that neither leaves nor flowers touch glass.

plants need moist air

Fresh and moist air are as necessary to the health of house plants as to people. Correct preparation of planters as described on page 26 helps in this problem. There are several other ways to achieve sufficient moisture in steam-heated houses and apartments. You can:

1. Buy specially made inexpensive pans which may be filled with water and placed on the top or back of radiators nearest your plants.

2. Borrow a shallow aluminum dish (like a pie pan) from your kitchen, fill with water, and place on radiator nearest plants.

3. If plants are placed in planter without vermiculite or perlite, place glass or narrow jar of water in corner of planter.

Plants need oxygen and carbon dioxide. Therefore, you should air the room in which they are growing each day when possible. Do not open windows directly on plants.

plants must have water

There are general rules on watering which I will discuss here. I have tried to be more specific in the following chapters. Be sure to water any plant before it wilts.

Two simple tests will help you know when your plants need water.

1. Press a dry fingertip on soil. If soil particles stay together, there may be no need for watering.

2. If a toothpick put into soil comes out clean, water is probably needed.

Watering plants from below by placing pots in larger pan or sink full of water is the best method. Water saturates roots and seeps to the top. This method obviously takes longer than watering from the top, so do make sure the plant has really been soaked. Do not allow pot to stand in deep water for more than an hour.

If watering from top, water thoroughly.

If daily watering does not seem enough,

repot plants into larger containers with more space for water.

It is easier to take care of your plants by daily watering, but frequency of watering depends upon many things: the size of the container and the plant, the type of soil, and general growing conditions. You will get into the correct rhythm of regular watering by noting whether the surface of the soil is dry before watering.

Use water at room temperature. Allow excess water to drain from container, when possible, before plant is set back in drip catcher.

Water all plants from top occasionally to prevent mineral build-up.

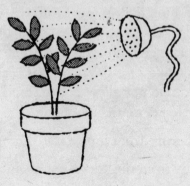

give the leaves a bath and a grooming

Wash the tops of most plants weekly with syringe or spray in sink. Hairy-leafed plants such as African Violets or Gloxinia should not be sprayed but should have their leaves brushed with a small camel-hair brush to remove dust. Plants breathe through their leaves, so they must be kept clean.

feeding

Plants should be fertilized regularly, usually monthly, with the exception of their resting period when they may need light, if any, feeding.

A liquid organic fertilizer is easiest. Follow the instructions on the bottle.

protection against pests

The best protection is to keep plants healthy by following the suggestions given in this chapter for the right atmosphere. In addition:

> Pick and throw away fallen leaves or old blooms.

> Spray plants gently with mild lukewarm water weekly.

> Do not use any of the commercial sprays because they are dangerous.

One of the most frequent pests is the "mealy bug," a small whitish creature. Dip a cotton swab in rubbing alcohol and gently clean off leaves and stems. A weekly spraying of mild soapy water should keep mealy bugs under control (2 tablespoons of soap flakes to 1 gallon of water and rinse thoroughly).

Should "scale" attack your plants, sponge with soap and water. Or if that fails, pick them off with a toothpick.

Cover top of pot with aluminum foil to protect soil from soapy water.

Do not waste your time on most house plants that continue to have diseases. Throw them away and start over. If the plant is valuable, consult the local horticultural organization for more detailed recommendations.

plants that cost very little

You can grow plants from some fruit seeds, like apples and oranges, and from the tops of some vegetables and fruits. Wonderful and strange shapes can come from such planting, but not fruit or vegetables.

Sometimes, however, nothing comes from it. I remember reading that "not every nut and seed that the birds and squirrels plant will grow." And so it is with our indoor planting.

But it is fun to experiment. Keep in mind that we cannot predict the way these plants will grow.

Here are some ideas to try and perhaps you will think of others.

plants from fruit seeds

here's what you need

Seeds from apples or lemons or oranges or grapefruit

4-inch flowerpot

Soil #1

here's what you do

1. Choose seeds that are plump. Wash and dry.

2. Prepare flowerpot according to instructions on page 23.

3. Label pot with name and date.

4. Fill with soil up to 1 inch from top.

5. Place several seeds of the same fruit 1 inch apart on surface of soil.

6. Cover with ¼ inch of soil.

7. Water carefully. Place in light or sunny spot.

8. Continue watering as needed.

9. Plants will develop in a time span ranging from 3 weeks to 3 months.

AVOCADO PLANT

There are two ways to start an avocado plant from the large seed in the center of the fruit. Perhaps you can acquire two seeds and try both methods at the same time and compare the results. These plants grow several feet high.

The first method (Plan A) gives an opportunity to watch the roots grow. The disadvantage is that avocado roots are tender and are often damaged in transplanting. The second method (Plan B) avoids that problem by planting directly in soil.

PLAN A

here's what you need

Avocado seed

Glass jar

Toothpicks or nails

5-inch pot

Soil #1

here's what you do

1. Fill glass jar about halfway with water.

2. Place 3 toothpicks, or nails, evenly around the top half of the seed.

3. Place larger, flattened end of seed downward in glass so that seed barely touches water. Pour out excess water. Maintain water at that level.

4. It is necessary for air to circulate. Seed should not completely fill jar opening.

5. After roots have formed (in about 4 weeks) prepare 5-inch pot for planting.

6. Make hole deep enough for seed and delicate roots without crushing. Place soil gently around seed and roots. Tamp down.

7. Keep in sunny window sill and water generously. When the plant is about 1 foot tall, pinch off top shoot and it will branch out at sides.

PLAN B

here's what you need
Avocado seed

5-inch pot

Soil #1

here's what you do

1. Prepare a 5-inch pot with good drainage per instructions, using regular potting soil.

2. Place the seed flattened end down—deep enough in soil to cover all except the tip.

3. Keep on window sill and water frequently until plant begins to grow, then increase watering.

4. When plant is about 1 foot high, pinch off top shoot and plant will branch out at sides.

   Avocados like plenty of light and humidity.

PINEAPPLE PLANT

If you know someone who buys whole fresh pineapples, ask him to save the top of a pineapple, keeping a thin slice of fruit attached. The pineapple plant that you grow at home will never have fruit, but it will have lovely green leaves and perhaps *may* blossom within a couple of years.

here's what you need

Shallow dish

Sand or perlite

Soil #2

Pineapple top

here's what you do

1. Slice off pineapple crown with about ¼ inch of fruit.

2. Remove row of lower leaves on the crown of the pineapple. Let crown dry for a day or two.

3. Plant top in about 1 inch of sand or perlite in dish.

4. Keep out of direct light and water plentifully until leaves appear.

5. Transplant into pot of Soil #2 and place in sunny window. Water as needed.

PEANUT PLANT

This is a fascinating plant if you can get it to grow. Yellow pea-like flowers send out long shoots that dig into the soil. It needs a lot of daylight.

here's what you need

6 or 8 unroasted peanuts, shelled

5- or 6-inch pot

Soil #1

here's what you do

1. Prepare pot according to instructions.

2. Place peanuts—placed far apart—into soil about 1 inch.

3. Keep moist and in as much light as possible.

> NOTE: You may want to buy peanuts in shells at the grocery store and then shell them. Or you can order peanuts from the seed catalog.

SWEET POTATO PLANTS

Sweet potato plants grow into pleasant-looking vines, if you can find a sweet potato that has not been coated with wax.

You can use either of the methods of planting suggested for the avocado plant. Once the plant begins to grow, a great many stems will appear. Take off all but 3 or 4 of the strongest.

CARROT PLANT

Leafy plants can be grown from carrot tops.

here's what you need

Shallow container

Sand or perlite

Several carrots

here's what you do

1. Cut off a ½ inch of carrot, keeping top.

2. Place sand in container and dampen.

3. Place carrot in sand or perlite with about ¼ inch of root showing.

4. Water frequently and leaves should begin to grow within a week.

> NOTE: Plants can be grown in the same manner from beets, turnips, and parsnips.

CLIMBING BEAN PLANT

here's what you need

4 or 5 scarlet runner beans

4-inch flowerpot

Small plastic or wood trellis

Soil #1

51

here's what you do

1. Prepare flowerpot following instructions.

2. Fill with about 3 inches of soil. Anchor small trellis.

3. Plant 4 or 5 beans, evenly spaced. You can speed up the germinating process by soaking the beans in warm water in a paper cup overnight.

4. Cover with ½ inch of soil.

5. Water carefully and place in light or sunny spot.

6. Continue watering as needed.

7. Young plants will appear within a few weeks. As the vines grow, they should be trained on the trellis. Red flowers may appear depending upon planting conditions.

> NOTE: You can start bean plants from other seeds that you will find listed in the catalog. Do not grow the castor bean plant because the seeds are poisonous.

things to keep in mind

To know how much soil to sprinkle over seed, the rule is: cover seeds with their own depth.

Do not let soil dry out. Water each day.

There are other seeds to be tried—olive, peach, mango—but their success is not so sure as the ones I have given.

You might try grape seeds, which produce a lovely vine. Soak seeds in water for a night and follow instructions for planting fruit seeds.

Date plants sometimes grow into nice little palms. It takes time and patience. The dates must be unpasteurized. Look at label.

chapter 4

flowering plants

Indoor blooming plants, with fresh colorful flowers, are pretty to see.

Before you choose a plant, consider the temperature and location. Most flowering plants need 3 to 5 hours of direct sunlight a day. Winter temperature in your house or apartment should average around 70° during the day and 60° at night.

Plants, like people, need a period of rest. Just as their watering needs are different, so are resting requirements.

Here is a list of plants that should grow and flower successfully for you:

1. Fibrous-rooted Begonias (also called Wax Begonias)

There are many varieties. The leaves are attractive as well as the flowers. Begonias need full sunlight in winter, partial shade in summer. They like warm temperature, Soil #1, and a moist atmosphere. Never let soil get dry.

New plants can be started from cuttings as described in Chapter 12. Each variety of Begonia needs different handling after it blooms so ask your nurseryman or florist for information.

2. Christmas Cactus

The foliage and shape are interesting. The blooms are delightful. Christmas Cactus is a short-day plant and it is necessary to keep it in complete darkness after 6 P.M. starting September 1. Development of buds for flowering will be helped by keeping plant in a cool temperature (around 40°). When buds are developed, plant may be moved back into room temperature. Keep in full sun during the winter. From May to

September, keep away from strong sunlight. The Christmas Cactus needs Soil #2 and a limited amount of water.

After it blooms, rest plant by keeping it nearly dry for 6 or 8 weeks. When new growth appears, repot or add fresh soil and water as before.

3. *Geraniums*

Geraniums are favorites because they bloom easily. They need a sunny but cool location with an ideal temperature of 50° to 60°. They grow well in Soil #1 and

should be fertilized a little more frequently than the other flowering plants. Water when soil is dry to the touch.

Cuttings from geraniums root easily and should be started early in the spring or fall.

4. Impatiens

You can have lovely fresh blooms of pink, lavender, rose, salmon, and scarlet red from Impatiens constantly through the winter.

Impatiens grow in full sunlight or in shade in Soil #1 with plenty of watering.

Prune in the spring and root cuttings at that time from pruned branches.

5. Fuchsia

This old-fashioned house plant is becoming popular again. There are many varieties so consult your nurseryman or florist.

Fuchsia grows well in full light, but not full sun. It needs Soil #1 with additional fertilizer, considerable water, and moisture.

flowering plants from seeds

Many attractive flowering house plants can be grown from seed including: Geranium, Impatiens, Lobelia, Dwarf French Marigold, and Sweet Alyssum.

One of our favorite flowering plants is a pepper plant, grown from seed. Since the seeds cost about 3½ cents apiece in a packet (or you can take them from the pepper itself), you can have plants for yourself and your friends. Plant the seeds as instructed and then transfer 1 or 2 seedlings to a 4-inch pot. Once you are certain that the plants will thrive, discard the smaller seedlings.

things to remember

Plants should be turned now and then to keep an even shape.

Pinch back to keep plants bushy.

With all flowering plants, remove faded blooms immediately.

It may be easier to keep a series of blooms with a number of small plants rather than one large plant.

flowering plants from bulbs

Bulbs can give beautiful flowers in winter when the outside world is often not attractive.

There are two general types of indoor bulbs. The fall-planted ones, like hyacinths, tulips, and daffodils, flower in winter and early spring. The winter-planted bulbs, like Amaryllises and Gloxinias, flower in late spring and summer. Certain varieties of Daffodil and Hyacinth, referred to as tender, need less time in the so-called "cold" period because they are precooled, or "tender."

When bulbs are grown indoors we use the word "forcing" because we are pushing their growth by placing them in a warm temperature more quickly than nature would have done outdoors.

Bulbs are planted in a loose crumbly soil or a special bulb mixture. Narcissi and Hyacinths, however, grow and flower equally well in water.

Start several plantings of bulbs at different times and you can have an indoor garden of flowering plants from January until late spring or early summer.

Keep plants away from intense heat.

NARCISSI
planted in water

here's what you need

3 to 5 plump Narcissus bulbs of "tender" variety

Dish or bowl about twice the depth of the bulb

Material such as pebble, gravel, or pearl chips

may be planted in early october

here's what you do

1. Fill bowl ⅔ full of material.

2. Place bulbs in material, flat or root side down. You may place them very close together, touching if necessary, in order to get a larger display.

3. Add water until it is even with top layer of material. Keep at this level.

4. Fill in with more material to hold bulbs upright, leaving top of bulb showing.

5. Place container in sunny window (though some experts suggest a cool dark place, even with the water method, until root growth has started).

Narcissi will flower in 3 to 5 weeks.

> NOTE: You may use a shallow bowl and place bulbs on top of material without surrounding them with additional material. I think the method given above makes a more attractive display, but either method should give you lovely flowers.

VARIETIES OF TENDER NARCISSI

Paper White

Chinese Sacred Lily—white with yellow center

Grand Soleil d'Or—yellow with orange yellow cup

HYACINTHS
planted in water

here's what you need

Large Hyacinth bulb

Hyacinth glass designed for purpose or jar that is suitable, such as chocolate flavoring jar.

here's what you do

1. Place bulb in cup on top of Hyacinth glass, or on top of any jar with an opening which will keep bulb suspended.

2. Fill glass or jar with water which is a hairline below bulb.

3. Place piece of aluminum foil loosely over bulb.

4. Keep glass in refrigerator or cold dark area until roots have grown—about 2

or 3 months for most varieties of Hyacinth.

Roman Hyacinths (which are pre-cooled or "tender") are particularly good for indoor forcing and root growth usually takes place in about 3 weeks.

5. Bring into light but cool area for a week or two.

6. After this period, place in room at normal temperature with average daylight.

CROCUSES, HYACINTHS, NARCISSI, TULIPS

here's what you need

Several bulbs of the variety you choose

4- to 5-inch flowerpots, bulb pans, or other containers

Soil #1 or bulb-planting mixture

PLANT IN LATE OCTOBER WHEN CON-
TINUED COLD WEATHER IS ASSURED. IF
USING REFRIGERATOR METHOD, YOU CAN
START IN LATE SEPTEMBER OR EARLY
OCTOBER.

here's what you do

1. Prepare pans or pots according to instructions for drainage.

2. Fill pot about ¼ full with soil.

3. Place bulbs—flattened, root side down
   —in container with pencil width between.

KEEP VARIETIES TOGETHER——TULIPS
IN ONE CONTAINER, CROCUSES IN
ANOTHER.

4. Cover with soil, leaving tip of bulb showing. Soil should be ½ inch below container line for easier watering.

5. Water thoroughly after planting. Continue to keep moist.

6. Label each pot with name, variety, time of planting.

    Hardy bulbs need a period of cold (40° temperature). Store in cold corner of basement, unheated closet, or wrapped in loose plastic bags in refrigerator.

7. After growth has appeared, move to light but cool area for several weeks.

8. Move to light and warmer area until flowers appear.

9. Continue to water plentifully while plant is growing and blooming.

    NOTE: Before bringing Tulips into warm location, sprouts should be at least 6 inches. Tulips seem to me to be the most difficult to cultivate indoors.

AMARYLLIS
(winter-planted from december to march)

here's what you need

Amaryllis bulb

6-inch pot

Soil #1 or bulb mixture

here's what you do

1. Prepare 6-inch pot according to directions.

2. Fill with Soil #1 about half way.

3. Place Amaryllis bulb and cover with soil leaving ⅓ of bulb exposed.

Remember to leave space for watering.

4. Water well the first time. Do not water again until the bulb shoot appears out of bulb neck. Once shoots begin, feed with liquid fertilizer.

5. Water lightly until bulb blooms. Flowers usually appear before leaves.

6. After bulb has flowered, water for a week or two to allow bulb to regain nourishment for next year. Then keep dry and let leaves die. Store in dark place in basement or cool closet until following January or until buds show. At that time "top dress," which means to scrape off top inch of soil in pot without disturbing bulb and substitute new soil containing complete fertilizer. Repot every third or fourth year.

GLOXINIA
(winter-planted)

here's what you need

Gloxinia bulb

5-inch pot

Soil #1 or bulb mixture

plant in january

here's what you do

1. Prepare 5-inch pot according to instructions.

2. Fill with soil up to 1 inch from top.

3. Place bulb, flat side down, about 1 inch below surface.

4. Water thoroughly, keeping water line below bulb.

5. When growth appears, feed with liquid fertilizer. Keep in daylight but not direct sun. Gloxinias should be kept away from light except weak early-morning and late-afternoon sunlight.

After flowering, water for a week or two, as with Amaryllis, to allow bulb to regain nourishment. Let dry off a month. Store bulb in basement or cool closet until next year.

things to remember about indoor bulb planting

Plant tender Narcissi or Roman Hyacinths in early October for Christmas or holiday bloom. If plants grow faster than planned, growth can be slowed by keeping plants in cool place away from light until about 2 weeks before holidays.

All indoor winter and early spring blooming bulbs are discarded after blooming. Bulbs will do well at blooming period by being in adequate daylight, but not direct intense sunlight.

Water level must always be a shade below bulb so that there is no danger of bulb rotting.

CALENDAR FOR GROWTH
IN SOIL

8 or more weeks for rooting at 40° F

3 or more weeks for growth of stems or leaves at 50° F

2 or more weeks for flower production at 60° F or above

Grow 3 to 5 bulbs of the same variety together, with the exception of the large Hyacinth, to have a better display of blooms. Containers should be twice as high as bulbs when grown in soil to allow for adequate root growth.

chapter 6

foliage plants

Foliage plants are usually grown for their beautiful leaves. They ordinarily do not have flowers and, generally, they are easier to grow than flowering plants. Most of them require an average soil mixture, the one we call Soil #1.

By "easier-to-grow" I mean that they adapt to the amount of light and heat and moisture that is available.

All these plants can be purchased, and you can start two of them—Asparagus Fern and Coleus—from seed. You can propagate them (start new plants from existing plants) as described in Chapter 12.

Here is a list for you to choose from:

1. Asparagus Fern has fine feathery foliage, but it is not really a fern.

It likes

> Ordinary light but manages with very little sunlight
> Considerable water
> Frequent applications of fertilizer

To start new plants: use the division method or start from seeds as described on package.

2. Aspidistra has marvelously large leaves. It is known as the "cast-iron" plant because it is so hardy.

It needs

> Plenty of water
> Thorough drainage in pot

To start new plants: use the division method in early spring.

3. Bromeliads have striking-looking foliage. They are known as "air plants" because they get most of their nourishment from air and water.

They need

    Either sun or shade
    Very little water

To start new plants: take leaf cutting.

4. Coleus has brilliant coloring and velvety-looking leaves. Sometimes it

blooms, but the flowers are small.

It likes

Lots of water, warmth, and light

It can be grown in water with occasional feeding. To start new plants: use stem cuttings and root in pots or water. After they are rooted, pot them and keep in sunny place.

5. Philodendron comes in many species, most with rich green leaves that are arrow-shaped. It can be grown as a climbing or trailing vine.

It likes

Shade
Moist but not oversoaked soil
To be kept pruned and neat, not straggly

To start new plants: use a stem cutting, after pruning, 4 to 6 inches long and root in sand or water.

6. Pickaback Plant has interesting foliage. It gets its name because little plants develop at the end of the leafstalk. They, in turn, produce smaller plantlets. Green flowers may appear, but they are not particularly pretty.

It likes

>Light but not bright sunlight
>Lots of water
>To grow in soil or water

To start new plants: pot leaves with small plantlets in tiny flowerpot. Can also be rooted in water.

7. Pothos is a vine with mottled leaves.

It likes

>Sun or ordinary light

To start new plants: root stem cuttings.

8. Rubber Plants have ornamental leaves.

They like

> Partial shade or sunlight
> A heavy soil (Soil #3)
> Fertilizer in early spring and summer

To start new plants: take stem cuttings. If these are not successful, you may find it necessary to buy additional plants.

chapter 7

indoor garden with plants that grow in water

If you cannot get soil, you can still have an indoor garden. There are indoor plants that grow well in water. Some, like Philodendron, for example, have many varieties. You will find enough contrast in color and size to make an attractive display.

here's what you need

One or two tall plants like Chinese Evergreen.

Medium-sized plants like Philodendron or Grape Ivy.

Several smaller vine-like plants such as English Ivy.

Containers of approximately the same height so that plants can be placed on one level.

Charcoal

Planter

These are three arrangements which lend themselves to these plants, but try others, if you prefer. Sketch your design first, keeping plants in mind.

ARRANGEMENTS

Crescent

Horizontal

Triangle

here's what you do

1. Choose or create your design. Draw on paper and mark where plants should be placed.

2. Fill containers with water. Add charcoal to keep water clean and avoid changing of water, which might damage roots.

3. Place plants in water and arrange in planter according to design. If you do not like one arrangement, try another.

The plants that I am suggesting have several things in common:

They

. . . are happy in the shade.

... do not need direct sunshine.*

... should be sprayed or washed with mild soapy water weekly.

... need liquid fertilizer monthly.

... should be pinched back to keep from getting straggly.

*Only the Philodendron can stand a small amount of direct sunshine.

chapter 8

indoor desert garden

You can have an unusual indoor garden by placing together a variety of cacti. Very few are "pretty" plants, but their rugged and individual looks are interesting. If conditions are right and the plants blossom, they are spectacular. Nursery plants are sometimes potted in an average mixture, but cacti thrive best in a sandier soil. It will probably be best to repot them.

Keep cacti in individual pots so that watering can be done to suit each plant. Different cacti have different moisture requirements.

indoor desert garden

here's what you need

One or two tall cacti (Cactus, Cereus; Cactus, Old Man; Cactus, Euphoria, or Snake Plant)

One or two medium-sized plants such as Kalanchoe, Panda Plant, Aurora Borealis Plant

Smaller plants such as Hen and Chickens, Sand Dollar

Soil #2

Planter

The arrangement that seems most appropriate is the L, but create your own design if you would like.

here's what you do

1. If plants need repotting, follow suggestions on page 106.

2. Sketch your design, filling in the plants for the right places.

3. Place in planter.

4. Keep in area where sufficient light is available.

5. Water well during growing season in late spring and summer.

THINGS TO REMEMBER ABOUT CACTI

Grow in sandy mixture.

Need fertilizer, well diluted, in late spring and summer—not winter.

Water lightly during growing season by

submerging pots almost to rims. Leave until water seeps through from bottom and wets surface soil.

Soil should be permitted to dry out in winter almost completely each time before watering.

Can stand a wide range of temperature.

Can do without sun but need sun to bloom.

Need daylight.

indoor rock garden

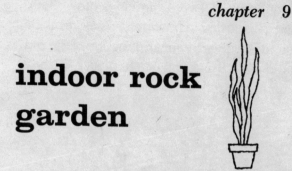

This miniature indoor garden should imitate, to some degree, natural rock formations. Plan in advance to get the plants and rocks.

Perhaps you can go rock hunting on day trips or on vacation. You can occasionally buy them at hobby or mineral shops. If possible, collect those of the same formation. Soft rocks (such as sandstone, limestone, or shale) are porous and coarse-grained, and store moisture. They are a good choice since we are trying to copy actual rock gardens.

Please do not feel discouraged if you can neither find nor buy rocks. You can have a type of "rock garden" with pieces of brick or concrete. Brick can be obtained at a lumberyard (even big cities have them) and discarded concrete pieces can be found frequently near new or very old buildings. Break up such pieces with a hammer into desired shapes.

Whatever you use, the major decision affecting the size and style of the planter you choose is: Can the drainage be handled within the planter (see page 26) or will there be an open drain?

If an open drain, the planter will need to be small enough so that it can be moved to the sink for watering, or positioned so that a container can be placed beneath the drain to catch excess water.

A rock garden needs to be steep and deep (at least 6 to 8 inches) and the size is important. The planter will be difficult to move around if too heavy.

here's what you need

1 foliage plant for background such as Velvet Plant or Snake Plant

1 or 2 medium-height plants for flowering such as French Marigolds or Thumbelina Zinnias

Sweet Alyssum

1 low-lying vine such as English Ivy or Smilax

Dampened brown peat moss

Gravel

Sand or perlite

Rocks

Soil #1

Planter

here's what you do

1. Choose rocks.

2. Scrub rocks with soap and water, using stiff brush. Rinse and dry.

3. Prepare planter:

   Place wide screening over drainage hole.

   Layer about 1 inch each of brown peat moss, gravel, sand, several inches of soil up to an inch from top.

   Place rocks in soil without disturbing layers.

   Let ⅓ of their height, like an iceberg, show. Tilt rocks to imitate natural rock formation.

   Add soil if needed to fill in between rocks. Tamp soil so that there will be no air pockets.

4. Choose a design for plants.

5. Place plants in position. Remember instruction on page 88.

THINGS TO KEEP IN MIND ABOUT ROCK GARDENS

Use plants of a species that by nature are small when fully grown.

Use two small plants rather than one large. Some grow more quickly and could change the balance of your garden.

Check soil condition frequently, especially in hot weather.

Nature would place taller plants at bottom of rock areas but in our miniature garden, small plants would then be hidden. Therefore, follow a design that places taller plants at side or back.

Most rock gardens need morning and evening sun, but should be sheltered from intense sun.

chapter 10

terrariums

A terrarium is an enclosed glass container in which a collection of similar plants are grown. It is particularly suited to plants that need a lot of moisture. Therefore, use it mainly for woodland and tropical plants. Do not combine them since they have different requirements.

If you wish to see the terrarium from all sides, put taller plants in center with smaller ones around. If terrarium will be seen from one side only, slope the moss and soil upward toward the back of the container. Use larger plants in back and smaller in front.

here's what you need

Clear glass container preferably with removable cover in order to control moisture in container—bowl, brandy snifter, bottle, aquarium.

Soil mixture that is porous and well drained—4 parts soil to 1 part peat moss with 1 level teaspoon of 5-10-5 fertilizer for every 2 quarts of soil mixture.

Drainage material—gravel, pieces of broken pots, sand, ground charcoal.

Tools such as wire rod, spoon, tweezers, cotton swab, sprayer or syringe.

Plant materials:

Wood moss from florist or woods

Small plants such as the following:

TROPICAL PLANTS

Ferns
Haworthia
Dwarf Coconut
Dracaena
Philodendron
Peperomia
Ardisia
Echeveria
Cryptanthus
Fittonia
Croton
Strawberry Begonia
Small-leaved Begonias

WOODLAND PLANTS

Ferns
Pipsissewa
Trailing Arbutus
Wintergreen
Rattlesnake Plantain
Hepatica
Wild Strawberry

Partridgeberry
Violets
Mosses
Shell Fungus
Seedling Evergreens

here's what you do

1. Line sides of container with moss, putting green side toward glass as high as you want soil to go.

2. Place ¼ to 1 inch of drainage material in flat bottom of container.

3. Add moistened soil up to height of moss sloping upward to give natural look.

4. Choose design. Arrange plants outside of terrarium to make certain design is effective before planting.

5. Scoop out holes large enough to receive balls of soil or cuttings.

6. Set plants and tamp soil gently around roots. Do not crowd plants or press against sides of container.

7. If roots are exposed, they will not dry out but will work themselves into soil.

8. Moisten soil lightly with bulb sprayer or syringe. Soil should be moist but not soggy. Spray off any particles of soil on leaves or walls of container.

9. Clean glass with paper tissue and place cover. Adjust cover so that there is a small opening for air movement.

> NOTE: You can make a cover out of transparent plastic wrap or aluminum foil.

CARE OF TERRARIUM

Keep in bright light but not direct sunlight.

Woodland terrarium should be kept in a cooler room than tropical one.

Water should be applied sparingly, a few teaspoons a month or less. Dig into soil with spoon to see if it is dry. Apply a small amount of water and recheck next day.

If you should overwater, remove cover and allow excess water to evaporate.

No additional fertilizer is necessary if it has been included in the soil mixture.

Remove dead leaves at once and prune or remove overgrown plants.

chapter 11

arrangement of plants

You are spending time and energy with your plants. It is important, therefore, to arrange them in a way which will display them best.

There are four things to keep in mind: design, scale, balance, and harmony.

DESIGN

A design is a plan of placing your plants. The following illustrations should be helpful whether plants are potted individually and placed on window sills, or grouped together in planters.

1. The crescent

2. The horizontal

3. The right angle

4. The circle

5. Vertical

SCALE

By scale, we mean selecting plants and containers that go together pleasingly to the eye. For example, you should not put several small cacti in a large delicate ceramic bowl. Instead, place them in a shallow rugged-appearing oval or crescent shape. Keep size of plants in proportion to other plants and container is the rule.

BALANCE

Balance in plant arrangement is a bit more difficult. It comes with practice. As you choose your design, think of the size and colors of your plants. Do not have a top-heavy look or too much of one color in the center. Small plants at the base of a planter, or along a window sill, help balance the total.

HARMONY

Put the right plants together, from the standpoint of season as well as color and variety.

starting new plants (propagation)

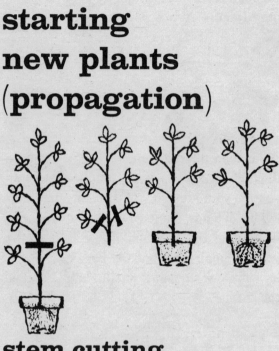

stem cutting

Cut off 4- to 6-inch stem at top just below the node, the point where leaf joins stem. Remove lower leaves. Place ⅓ of stem in vermiculite, perlite, or sand in small pot. Keep moist. Pot in 4-inch pot when roots form.

leaf cuttings

Cut off leaf with small part of stem. Root in sand, vermiculite, or water. Keep moist. Pot when roots form.

For some succulent plants (Sansevieria), take leaf off, do not bruise. Insert leaf into sand that is barely damp. Young plant forms at base of leaf. When roots are grown and little leaf is big enough to handle, it will come away from the original leaf and be ready to pot.

division

Plants that make several crowns, like Ferns and Aspidistra, may be divided. Remove plant from pot. Shake off loose soil. Remove any dead roots. Divide crowns by carefully pulling apart.

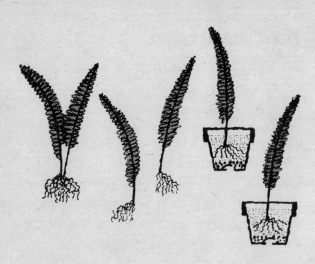

Hold plant in one hand, place it low in pot while gradually adding soil with other hand. With each addition of soil, gradually raise plant until its crown is 1 inch below rim of pot.

Tamp soil and water thoroughly.

runners

Long, leafless strands known as "runners" grow from some plants like the Pickaback Plant. Peg or pin runner to soil in small pot placed by large plant. Roots will form quickly and may then be potted up in right size container.

from seeds

Follow instructions on package and plant seeds in sterilized soil or sterile material such as vermiculite or shredded sphagnum moss in seed pans or shallow boxes. Cover lightly and keep evenly moist.

As soon as seedlings appear, give plenty of light and reasonably cool temperature (65°). Transplant to pots when large enough to handle.

Seeds sprout within 1 to 3 weeks, and most of the plants take from 6 to 9 months to bloom.

> NOTE: Whatever method you choose for starting new plants, label the container with plant name and date of propagating.

repotting

Potted plants from greenhouses usually have sufficient soil to supply their needs for several weeks. Eventually they need shifting to larger pots as do your regular house plants.

Plants which are not shifted to larger pots often have stunted growth and therefore become less attractive.

Follow this procedure:

1. Have supply of pots ready. (Remember that old ones should be scrubbed and dry. New porous clay pots should be soaked at least an hour.) Size should be no more than 2 inches larger than presently used.

2. Follow the drainage procedure on page 23.

3. Have soil mixture ready.

4. To remove plant and soil ball, turn pot upside down. Place hand on soil so base of plant is between index and middle fingers.

5. Tap rim of pot on edge of workbench. Pot should slide out easily.

6. Remove old drainage material if it clings to soil ball, and gently force roots apart with fingers. This lets roots reach fresh soil for nourishment.

7. Place plant in center of pot, holding on to it. Add soil gradually, packing firmly but gently with fingertips so that there are no large air spaces.

8. Soil surface should be ¼ to ½ inch below rim for efficient watering.

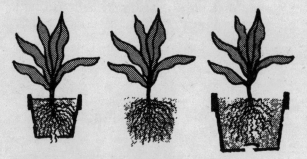

top-dressing

Instead of repotting, you may top-dress a plant. Remove the upper 2 inches of soil, including roots, and replace with fresh potting soil. This is particularly useful for a very large plant, which could be difficult to repot.

artificial light for plants

If you do not have sufficient daylight in your house or apartment, you can still grow plants indoors by artificial light. Daily care, with particular attention to watering, is very important.

Ordinary 60- or 75-watt incandescent bulbs can be placed above nonflowering house plants like Pothos and Philodendron in a dark part of the room for 4 to 6 hours a day.

Simple fluorescent light units are available which will help all varieties to grow. However, most flowering plants need a combination of some daylight and fluorescent lighting to complete their growing cycle— that is, to set buds and bloom.

The use of special horticultural fluorescent tubes will allow plants to complete their growing cycle without any daylight.

Complete lighting units can be purchased. They may include a reflector and a tray and are adjustable in height. You will find units described in most seed and garden catalogs. Sylvania Gro-Lux is one of the most popular.

If you are old enough, and ambitious, you can build an entire indoor garden unit made up of a planter and equipped with high intensity fluorescent lamps. You will need a licensed electrician and you must make certain that the wiring meets the local and the National Electrical codes. Write to the U.S. Department of Agriculture, Washington, D.C., or your local County Agricultural Agent for Home and Garden Bulletin No. 133, "Indoor Gardens for Decorative Plants."

I am sure that I need not remind you to group together those plants whose needs are the same.

Plants should be placed from 10 to 12 inches from the light. Some adjustment may be required, depending upon the height of the plant. If the leaves curl, the light is too close; if the stems grow too long, the light is too far away.

Leave fluorescent lights on 12 to 14 hours a day and adjust the schedule according to the needs of your plants. Remember that a period of darkness is necessary.

chapter 14

where to get further information

A County Agricultural Agent is located in most counties at the town called the county seat. He, or someone in his office, will give you advice on gardening problems by phone or by letter. Look up the county in the phone book and under that you will find the County Agricultural Agent.

If you are in a large city that has a botanical garden, they too will give you information by phone or by letter.

In each state, the Agricultural College and the Extension Service publish information on gardening, and a list of available material will be sent if you ask for it.

The bulletins and booklets are free to residents of the state.

Alabama: Auburn University, Auburn
36820

Alaska: University of Alaska, College
99701

Arizona: University of Arizona, Tucson
85721

Arkansas: University of Arkansas,
Fayetteville 72701

California: University of California,
Berkeley 94720

Colorado: Colorado State University,
Fort Collins 80521

Connecticut: University of Connecticut,
Storrs 06268

Delaware: University of Delaware,
Newark 19711

Florida: University of Florida, Gainesville
32601

Georgia: University of Georgia, Athens
30601

Hawaii: University of Hawaii, Honolulu
96822

Idaho: University of Idaho, Moscow 83843

Illinois: University of Illinois, Urbana
61801

Indiana: Purdue University, Lafayette
47907

Iowa: Iowa State University, Ames 50010

Kansas: Kansas State University,
Manhattan 66502

Kentucky: University of Kentucky,
Lexington 40505

Louisiana: Louisiana State University,
Baton Rouge 70803

Maine: University of Maine, Orono 04473

Maryland: University of Maryland,
College Park 20740

Massachusetts: University of Massachusetts, Amherst 01002

Michigan: Michigan State University,
East Lansing 48823

Minnesota: Institute of Agriculture, University of Minnesota, St. Paul 55455

Mississippi: Mississippi State University,
State College 39762

Missouri: University of Missouri,
Columbia 65201

Montana: Montana State University,
Bozeman 59715

Nebraska: College of Agriculture, University of Nebraska, Lincoln 68503

Nevada: University of Nevada, Reno
89507

New Hampshire: University of New
    Hampshire, Durham 03824
New Jersey: State College of Agriculture,
    Rutgers University, New Brunswick
    08903
New Mexico: New Mexico State Univer-
    sity, Las Cruces 88001
New York: New York State College
    of Agriculture, Cornell University,
    Ithaca 14850
North Carolina: North Carolina State
    University, Raleigh 27607
North Dakota: North Dakota State
    University, Fargo 58102
Ohio: The Ohio State University,
    Columbus 43210
Oklahoma: Oklahoma State University,
    Stillwater 74074
Oregon: Oregon State University,
    Corvallis 97331
Pennsylvania: Pennsylvania State Uni-
    versity, University Park 16802
Puerto Rico: University of Puerto Rico,
    Rio Piedras 00931
Rhode Island: University of Rhode Island,
    Kingston 02881

South Carolina: Clemson University,
Clemson 29631

South Dakota: South Dakota State
University, Brookings 57006

Tennessee: University of Tennessee,
Knoxville 37916

Texas: Texas A&M University, College
Station 77843

Utah: Utah State University, Logan 84321

Vermont: University of Vermont,
Burlington 05401

Virgin Islands: Virgin Islands Agricultural
Project, Kingshill, St. Croix 00850

Virginia: Virginia Polytechnic Institute,
Blacksburg 24061

Washington: Washington State University,
Pullman 99163

West Virginia: West Virginia University,
Morgantown 26506

Wisconsin: The University of Wisconsin,
Madison 53706

Wyoming: University of Wyoming,
Laramie 82070

glossary

Soil is a combination of physical, chemical, and other forces acting on minerals and organic things.

Humus is an important part of soil. It is a dark-brown substance resulting from the decomposition of plant or animal residues. For indoor gardening, we use peat moss.

Sphagnum peat moss (which we call "brown" peat moss throughout the book) is humus resulting from moss.

Fertilizer is a carrier of essential nutrient elements. Organic fertilizers, like bone meal or liquid fish fertilizer, are natural fertilizers which come from plant or animal substances.

Perlite is crushed volcanic rock that helps

to absorb excess moisture in soil. It serves the same purpose as coarse or sharp sand, which is often hard to find or buy.

Pinch back is the term used for a mild pruning in which you remove the growing point of a plant and thereby cause the plant to stop its growth upward and spread out.

Vermiculite is crushed mica, a mineral which is light in weight and holds moisture.

Index

121

29584 MINE FOR KEEPS, by Jean Little. Illustrated by Lewis Parker. Sally overcomes the handicap of cerebral palsy by reaching out to a new world of friendship, trust, and love when she moves home to live with her family and go to public school. (75¢)

29801 JENNY, by Gene Inyart. Illustrated by Nancy Grossman. Jenny's summer is full of happy surprises as she makes friends with the new family next door, and finally gets the puppy that she has always wanted. ($1.25)

29769 A SPELL IS CAST, by Eleanor Cameron. Illustrated by Beth and Joe Krush. Cory is drawn deep into a mystery when she tries to unlock the secret behind the strange, unhappy atmosphere at Tarnhelm. ($1.25)

29770 PERPLEXING PUZZLES AND TANTALIZING TEASERS, by Martin Gardner. Illustrated by Laszlo Kubinyi. A fascinating collection of puzzles and teasers to challenge your wits, tickle your funny bone, and give you and your friends hours of entertainment. (95¢)

29746 KIDS COOKING: *A First Cookbook for Children,* by Aileen Paul and Arthur Hawkins. Easy to prepare recipes for desserts, party foods, snacks, breakfast, lunch, and dinner dishes are included in this basic guide to the fun of cooking for girls and boys. ($1.25)

29778 THE HOUSE OF THIRTY CATS, by Mary Calhoun. Illustrated by Mary Chalmers. Adventure and excitement enter Sarah's life when she pays her first visit to Miss Tabitha's wonderful house, meets the members of the cat community, and chooses a kitten of her very own. ($1.50)

29740 THE TRUE STORY OF OKEE THE OTTER, by Dorothy Wisbeski. Illustrated with photographs. The beloved pet of a suburban family, Okee is a happy-go-lucky clown, curious about everything, and in and out of mischief. ($1.25)

29638 THE SPIDER PLANT, by Yetta Speevack. Illustrations by Wendy Watson. When urban renewal forces her family to move to an uptown project, Carmen isn't sure she will like it. But she soon finds that she can make friends and have fun in her new neighborhood. (75¢)

29627 KIDS CAMPING, by Aileen Paul. Illustrated by John DeLulio. This practical book contains all the vital information you need as a beginning camper, including chapters on buying equipment, where to go camping, pitching a tent, menus, and safety measures. (75¢)

(If your bookseller does not have the titles you want, you may order them by sending the retail price, plus 35¢ per book for postage and handling to: Mail Service Department, POCKET BOOKS, a division of Simon & Schuster, Inc., 1 West 39th Street, New York, N. Y. 10018. Please enclose check or money order—do not send cash.)

29608